I Climb the Mesas

Also by
Paula Gunn Allen

Blind Lion

Coyote's Daylight Trip

A Cannon Between My Knees

Shadow Country

The Sacred Hoop: Recovering the Feminine in American Indian Traditions

Wyrds

Skin and Bones

Life Is a Fatal Disease: Collected Poems 1962–1995

America the Beautiful: Last Poems

I Climb the Mesas

Selected Poems of

Paula Gunn Allen

RE LIT

Montclair | Amsterdam | Hoboken

This is a ReLIT book

Published by Levine Querido

www.levinequerido.com • info@levinequerido.com
Levine Querido is distributed by Chronicle Books, LLC

Library of Congress Control Number: 2024950902

ISBN 978-1-64614-582-9

Printed and bound in China

MIX
Paper | Supporting responsible forestry
FSC™ C144853

Published in November 2025

First printing

CONTENTS

FOREWORD

My mother, Paula Gunn Allen, was on the move for most of my life. While I was growing up, we never lived anywhere for more than two years. Most of the relocating was due as much to her academic pursuits and economic needs as it was to her restless, curious nature. That dynamic changed when she moved to Fort Bragg, California, in 2001, where she lived until she died in 2008. Until then I had never known her to stay in the same place seven years in a row.

I'm here in Fort Bragg, writing this foreword, in the very room where my mother typed up her final poems for her last book of poetry, *America the Beautiful*, published posthumously in 2010. This room is the same one where my brother, sister-in-law, and a few very close friends and I gathered while Paula made her journey to the Ancestors.

Throughout all that moving around, Mom always encouraged me to read, read, read. She usually had two or three books going at the same time at home, and even more in her office at school. She was often working on some writing project or another, quite a lot of it poetry. She had an indefatigable desire to explore and define the world and life through words.

And Paula was always teaching. That's how she supported her family, yet it was more than a job. So much of the work she did in and outside of academia was focused on examining cultural identities and their intersections within society. Mom taught people, including me, how to find and express their own stories, identities, and voices through words; she taught in the classroom and by example.

Paula used to describe herself as a multicultural event. She had an inherent understanding—or ideal, if you will—that cultural identities can be very different from one another physically and spiritually, while still being able to live alongside each other, and that in fact they could help one another thrive.

I Climb the Mesas: Selected Poems of Paula Gunn Allen demonstrates the passion with which Mom explores and defines life's multifaceted complexities. I deliberately use the present tense, because although she has passed from corporeal form, Paula's words continue to prod the reader into exploring the depths of their own cultural identities and experiences. She challenges us to be vulnerable, to be strong, to be angry, to grieve, to laugh, to love, and to see things from others' perspective. In a very real way, Paula is still on the go and continues to enthrall and amaze me. Thanks to Levine Querido for facilitating this leg of her journey.

—**LAURALEE BROWN**

INTRODUCTION

Memorializing a renowned family member is often difficult. Where do you start? With their impact in the world? Their incredible intellectual capacity? The eloquence of their words? Or with the quieter moments of conversation and laughter? The music and games in a flat in San Francisco? It's a delicate balance, but I guess I'll start with a journey.

When I was thirteen. my grandparents came to live with us in what would be the last year of my grandmother's life. Auntie Paula moved in down the block to be closer to her parents (both of whom are omnipresent in this collection). Before that, we moved my grandparents from Las Vegas. On that trip home, I got the chance to ride with Auntie in her fresh convertible. The drive across the desert to Southern California is indelibly etched into my brain because it was a moment to really get to know my Auntie one on one. Laughing and spinning stories, she told me about her time growing up and her love for her parents. We enjoyed the sunshine and wind in our hair. Four hours later, and too soon, the trip was over. Of course, many know her by her influential Indigenous feminist writings and her polemics on colonization and mixed identity but this drive was my Auntie the poet.

Kahlil Gibran once wrote, "Poetry is a deal of joy and pain and wonder, with a dash of the dictionary." This was and is the essence of my Auntie. Her life was moments of both joy and pain, stirred in a multicultural stew of Arabic and Indigenous, German and New Mexican. From her childhood in Cubero to the loss of her children, she brought her full self, her heart, her wisdom, her sorrow, her triumphs to each line, verse, stanza.

In her poetry, you experience her family, her joy, her journey through a most incredible life. Her words illuminate, as all good poetry does, the things that were most intimate and meaningful, not just for her but also for the readers of those words. Even though she never told me directly, I believe she felt the role of the poet was to share the personal and the magical, and to bring that magic to the world. It is amazing to read her poetry now that I am about the same age as she was when she lived down the street and to understand so much about my life through her reflections and insight.

After the passing of my grandmother, we moved to the East Coast and Auntie moved as well. We didn't connect much after that, but I was aware of her continued scholarship and writings, and was always proud to talk about her in my academic settings. As she was influential for so many people through her profound understandings, she was influential for me through her stories of our family and our heritage. She passed away in 2008, five years after my father crossed over and seventeen years after her own mother. There are many things that I remember and reflect on these days and I still have her early chapbooks and seminal works of my bookshelves. The memories drift this way and that but I still remember that drive.

And I can still hear her laughter.

—LEE FRANCIS IV

I Climb the Mesas

Snowgoose

North of here where
water marries ice,
meaning is other than what
I understand.

I have seen in picture how
white the bulge of the glacier
overshadows the sea,
frozen pentecostal presence,
brilliant in the sun—
way I have never been.

I heard the snowgoose cry today
long-wheeled wings overhead,
sky calling untroubled blue
song to her and morning.
(North wind blowing.)

The Kerner Report on Camp Creek Road

even bright as he is
he is dead: red flowered
the black skin, shattered
the white bone. He is
free.

as so they form a club
and meet each week to purge
themselves but not of grief,
idling over scotch and hors
d'oeuvres, assuring each and all
have at some time been good
to a "colored person." All
fear the brightening truth
that stalks the beige livingrooms
and will soon become its own
televised scream.

now whispering only in the softness
of the women's expensive shifts, blowing
out the doors with the grey smoke, bubbling
in Alka-Seltzer which will end the blahs.
What can we wring from our powdered perfumed power
less hands they ask each other over

after all we can't very well scream
or be unmanly what
do they want we cannot build houses or minds
at a time like this we have all earned all
it takes is grim determination

when he was shot the cops
cordoned off the Memphis ghetto
Take the full length of a club
and a street of people crying;
tie them together to make
a journey as long as a night of rot.
Put them carefully in a warm, dark place.

(when he was shot the cops
cordoned off the Memphis
ghetto)

If I had a metaphorical knife
and a metaphorically thick cutting board
and a whole pile of translucent metaphors
I would slice them finely and watch
them quiver in the light:

white underside of that big fish
slit open, guts expertly removed,
breakfast in clean pine air, no
trace of odor but pine. Go now,
while the sun is still shining.

Displacement

I mean
it's big industry
twelve million pounds
apochryphal.
And despair has no solution,
the drunk little man said.
They were done:
all little things
now done, and in a BIG WAY
over miles disproportionate and stupifying.
Flounder found too far from the water it was born in,
frozen now and super-merchandized:
and nothing stays in any sense where it belongs.

The pain is simply in the sense
of the identity with place.
And history is a question of where to die
or where to go to be buried
when no place is home
(the corpses lie at rest in impersonal mortuaries
and the community of novelties
in the continuity of space
makes wherever it happens to be

the place of use: not
in the sense of home—
the children might not wish to stay—.
The severing of bonds is hard.
But ties are not the only pain that breaks.

Coyote's Daylight Trip

Poled to its environment, shored,
an imagined thing made by hand does not connect—
senses of accuracy in the machine are light
etched on paper,
means:

BRINGING HOME THE FACT

Men each day go out, return, though mourning the sight:
questions posed in photographs, whether of the mind or not.
And loony poor Bud deranges life; all literature a spindly bough
that cannot hold true, Sapling grown in spring is gone in snow—
disactualized.

HISTORY HAPPENS

How it comes chemical, charged, is no matter
of fact but Photograph and
Type. Did they make pictures of Calley's, Ellsberg's
damaged psyche? I
am inconsequential as the wind. No
picture can be made of formulations called myself: mere
corpses show on the plate, true as fact, grow
monstrous in every quiet place, an
institution.

I SEE MYSELF AS DEATH

Vapors play poorly in the light, leave tracings that once swam
onto the page and fixed themselves through careful eye: I
cannot care for this—ancestor's shades fixed on the wall.
I bury my dead. I mourn
for four full days.

Woman's Day 1975

We drove for a long time twisting along the city
like an old hem, torn and dirty from the wear.
I sat in the back
facing where we had been. The highway
spun out from under me like a spider's thread, and the air
grew heavier as we moved south toward Moffett Field.
We stopped at the gate, no pass, phone call, permission
to enter—car full of women set to tell
the ultimate enterprise that woman was at last awakening,
blinking in the dirty air, like a goddess as yet undreamed.
I sat tucked among the vast grey buildings one
transfixed in time. The Wind Tunnel, someone said.
It hung like doom between two buildings.
We drove across the air field.
"Watch for low-flying planes," said, laugh, lost momentarily.
"Do they make wind in that tunnel?" I asked: no one laughed.
We passed a crumpled airforce jet, slim nose crushed
against a 1963 Ford Falcon facing it. "They sure don't
make planes like they used to."
The air is cobweb, used, abandoned dream
fallen into silence, left to brood about its dead,
all systems clogged, it hangs brown and sullen over us
as we drive south
awakening.

Moonshot: 1969

Had nothing to do on Wednesday
but watch the house grow hot and silent
in the heat. The dust on the TV and under the couch
looks muggy. The cat and I sleep, hot, waiting for dark.

The moon is still more imagination than rock. It is said
that two men have at last soared beyond the heat and noise—
blood no longer heavy
head, hands, heart
light
beyond our sight if not the subtle hearing of the grounded
quick-fingered machines.
But I love you.
How equate the moonlight falling
soft across your shoulders with ash and stone
so deceptively light, impossibly cohesive?
Where they are is not where we have been.

When I say moon
I do not mean the dark, pretty hulk
45,000 miles out there, but moon:
heart, a quiet cool house;
children breathing dreams,
whimpering sometimes to their visions;

moon: a light softly centering inside my eyes:
no one can land there where there is no land
and the air too vague
to provide footing to luminous ghosts;
moon: spirit of the spirit's strength;
moon: wandering pale forests,
springing out of undefinable lost impulse,
hunting through networks more complex than all
buzzing, humming technocracies of Washington, Houston,
Flagstaff. . . .

The Source of that light was lost ages ago,
but still spreads toward me, trembling at the edges of my eyes
always threatening to break through.
Not 90 million miles outside of me, but inside,
that light,
frozen on
that moon,
that I do not see so much as remember
as a feeling is remembered: never touched or seen but
heard, in echoing, aching moon dreams.

The idea was not that gazing at the moon
        (now another base, the outer edge of our expansion,
        that moon that is cratered and carved
        volcanic rock, meteor pocked
        that circles predictably as our machines circle us)
would drive a woman insane. Gazing at an object,
however distant, cannot drive a woman anywhere,
certainly not over to the far reaches of visioning

where the real is incommunicable and so thought
by strangers
not to exist, but gazing into the moon reaches of the mind,
searching with careful fingers of sense-memory,
listening inside the ear for lost songs,
almost forgotten footfalls,
feeling gingerly with the tongue-tip of the heart—
this gazing, steady, frightened, is the scape of moon madness,
the certain consequence of remembering
what is best forgot.

On television I hear them say
that because man has landed on the moon
he has laid forever its tidal pull on the heart to rest.
Outside my bedroom window, late, I sleep and wake
and sleep again,
feel the soft light fall on my face,
see its evanescent glow polish your shoulders, back, buttocks,
the lined and wrinkled bottom of your moonward sole
to the dull mysterious lustre;
I wake, sleep, dream.

Zen Americana

Un is okay.
Un pretentious. Un decided. Un known.
Un ego is where I want to be. How do you open
the door to Un? What does the un place look like,
look alikes?

Un beginning; can I un wake myself, un sleep
motionless in a bright green chair?
Maybe un lamps light the room (the un place).
When I get there, maybe it will be dark, un lit
where it has no occasion to be any way.

(Un celebrated.)
(Un repentant.)
(Un regenerate.)
(Un believed.)

The Trick Is Consciousness

I must have been mistaken.
Taken for a ride, an eternity of them,
masked strangers driving me hundreds of miles in
unidentifiable cars down nameless highways,
dark sideroads of a thousand tales and thoughts—I
must have misunderstood the terms of the agreement
between time and place, identity and surmise, those roads
led somewhere, I thought, and those someones would take me
swiftly there. I must have been wrong.
It has, I suppose, to do with temporality—
sensation, duration, whatever we know of time:
with how waves swell and break, how sand blows from one
county to the next, how light blooms pale and deep
one year from another, yet still remains the light.
I think about long ago
as they say or said humma ho when the tale began,
and wonder how the earth has changed, not I but
it in twenty years, wonder at the completeness of it,
getting, forgetting, sudden realization, no
excuses, no surprise,
there it is.

I remember the corral behind the house,
the wooden stairs up to it, chicken house, stall, rabbit pen,

pigeon pen, the high rocks shading.
It was full during the war. My father
didn't want us to want—there were chickens, rabbits, a cow
that gave enough for the whole village, sheep, pigeons,
a huge pig.
They made chicharrones when they slaughtered it.
I was maybe four.
Later the corral was empty.
Used to wander around in it, wondering.
I still do, at night, at dream.
And I remember grandma's mulch bed—
the crazy lily pond she ran us out of,
the tamarack tree behind the coal shed, deep
shadows there, spider webs, trumpet vine, I
dream about them now, sound, smell, shade and light
so complete—I have changed nothing.

The key is in remembering, in what is chosen for the dream.
In the silence of recovery we hold
the rituals of the dawn,
now as then.

Watch

The cycle grows impassable.
To be beholden.
Uncomprehending but beheld.
I think of dawn in July,
watched from the mesa behind my house,
the still purple village groping toward light,

sky on fire
not in metaphor
clouds billows of smoke:
I didn't know then what it signified, but I watched,
still,
shivering in the quick cold air. I was twelve.
In full daylight the mountains were pale,
the long sunbitten afternoons
were and still are uncomprehended in their completeness,
consummate wish somehow buried
in the space of time passing
gone before our eyes, that yesterday.
Nobody goes down the old highway in wagons anymore.

But they did.

Wind in early morning, June, the perfect smell of clarity.
Did you know that the trees were gold then,
the light was, no explanation for it, but there it was.
The free air coming in the window.
Trick of sunlight? Trick of eyes?
It doesn't do that anymore. No tricks this time.
The trees showered light like clouds shower water.
Four summers or more it was that way, all
the times I woke in summer. No matter what
color my room was painted.
It was like that since I was a baby.
So there is that.
Childhood holds such mystery. I live it over and over—
at night, in sleep, during the day,

watching
waking.
Those trees were mystery.
When you looked you knew they were green,
though your mind held gold, holds it still.
Behind them stood the sky, silent accomplice to their will.
The bark was rough and silvery.
Grandma didn't like those Chinese elm trees, I
couldn't understand why. We would sit lazy crooked
in the branches,
chattering through long afternoons, trying to read the clouds.
How could we know then what is so plain to us now?

Control is out of reach.
We knew that then.
As now we know that outside these lighted islands of our lives
the dark is growing
hurtling toward us at the speed of light.

Grandmother

Out of her own body she pushed
silver thread, light, air
and carried it carefully on the dark, flying
where nothing moved.

Out of her body she extruded
shining wire, life, and wove the light
on the void.

From beyond time,
beyond oak trees and bright clear water flow,
she was given the work of weaving the strands
of her body, her pain, her vision
into creation, and the gift of having created,
to disappear.

After her,
the women and the men weave blankets into tales of life,
memories of light and ladders,
infinity-eyes, and rain.
After her I sit on my laddered rain-bearing rug
and mend the tear with string.

Creation Story

Light.
Stage of dawn.
Opening on new worlds
for the fifth time.
And not until they came forth
the Fourth Time was it ripe.
That dawn She came,
riding the sun,
humpback flute player heralding Her dawn
the Corn, sweet maiden, riding
the new day
latest in a series
of alternate paths
time of colors
rising.
And the sign of those days would be 4
She decreed, and the people arising
agreed. So we emerged into consciousness.
Born below in the place of nourishment
where those who have gone
wait, work, and come four days at a time
bringing the rain, coming home.
They fall on the gentle earth, sighing,
the squash, bean, corn sing of growing

and of grace. Pollen on the air golden
in that time, glowing, that return.
So on that day was given all this,
called Iyetiko, called Mother,
the clans, the people, the deer:
tracks left here and there
are signs.

Deep Deep City Blues:
Elegy for the Man Who Owned the Rain

On such a day
troubled waters gurgle in my chest:
pericarditis I suppose they'd say,
though the clouds probably
see it otherwise as they twist and stammer in the sky.
Cold wind kicks up dust, smells of rain.
Inevitably, the mesas (aloof) call to me.
Invariably, I can't go to them—such
is the nature of our understanding—
like high pressure zones and cool air flows
twist and stutter in my chest, unmediated,
unreturned: the dead from broken jars remain, unreborn.
No name I say can find its object here: trouble
needs no name. The sandy plateaus speak
their own-way language, and dry gullies
gurgle emptiness on to the barren plains.
(Coyote caverns haunt the mounds and
Thunder-hollows curve around the mind
to bend it to their will.)

It will rain again tonight.
Then the clouds will be able to be still.

Relations

underside of a dead sperm-whale.
underside of the rocks of eternity.
underside of moons, cannibal-lovers of all the earths.
underside of knowing and care.
upturned belly of rotting muse.
white, decaying fibers of mountains, upturned.
underside of clouds.
underside of lakes.
underside of dead sperm-whales.
of dead poets, dead buffalo, dead coyotes, dead waters, dead
    ground,
where understanding hangs in the balance,
precariously. underside of the hanged man.
underside of the hermit.
underside of the fool.
underside of the sun. the moon. the stars
where wise-men look down from the tower at the upturned belly
    of earth.
cántas encantadas, wondering, de la luna, del sol, del muerte,
de la vida
(forgotten and lost) where song is a one-time shot, where
pain and bearing in blood make the herb of understanding bloom
on this once new earth that is dying once again:

the star of yesterday came this way, unseeing. ignorant
of its own meaning, it went by, light of a corpse dead
fifty million light-years ago or more, saying: I tasted this earth once,
and so I know. I speak, I pass, I will not believe, I will go.

Two

FOR VINE DELORIA JR.

In the winter everything disappears
leaving a lonely bird or two
and some dry stalks of last year's grass.
Another time: mutuality, kindness—and
lords who could still display themselves to fire,
remembering somehow in that celebration the
Law, the
Winter, the
long flight of moon in the dry sky.

It is autumn strangely here.
We know season by recall—
and this is how we celebrate
the beloved whose lost voice cries
soundless
at the sphere of reflected light.

In tribal dreams
image and sound together make complicated song,
dancing wheels of air trace our spiraling path,
birds lost to the emptiness of sky. We
simply follow disappearance over
each next rise, but

this winter, or that, we shall go home again,
back to our own time and earth,
and know again the changelessness,
the silence, the
strong
sure steps of home.

Powwow 79, Durango

haven't been to one in almost three years
there's six drums and 200 dancers a few
booths piled with jewelry and powwow stuff
some pottery and oven bread
everyone gathers
stands for the grand entry
two flag songs
and the opening prayer by some guy
works for the BIA
who asks our father
to bless our cars
to heal our hearts
to let the music here tonight
make us better, cool
hurts and unease
in his son's name, amen.
my daughter arrives, stoned,
brown face ashy from the weed,
there's no toilet paper
in the ladies room she accuses me
there's never any toilet paper
in the *ladies* room at a powwow she glares
changes
calms

it's like being home after a long time
are you gonna dance I ask
here's my shawl
not dressed right she says
the new beaded ties I bought her swing
from her long dark braids
why not you have dark blue on I say
look.
we step inside the gym
eyes sweep the rubber floor
jackets, jeans, down-filled vests,
sweatshirts all dark blue.
have to look close to pick out
occasional brown or red on older folks
the dark brown faces rising on the bleachers
the dark hair on almost every head
ever see so many Indians
you're dressed right
we look at the bleachers
quiet like shadows
the people sit watching the floor below
where dancers circle the beating drums
exploding color in the light.

Crow Ambush

(Song for '76)

crow
circling overhead
stands on a broken branch
to consider his reflection
in the pool

moon
riding herd on utility poles
wonders
when the converging lines
will surround him

wind
lulling grass into submission
mutters to the drying hills
(eating pemmican)

nothing obvious
a natural sort of understanding
elusive as half-meant charity as
singing a boarding-school song
from Indian 49:

"HII-AA HA HA HAA. HII-AA HA HA HAA.
I'd rather be a drunkard than a fool."

Que Cante Quetzal

FOR ROBERTO VARGAS

I heard an expert say that the revolution is over;
but they're napalming Indians in Brazil.
The dead bear witness to the present in Wounded Knee.
In Bolivia, the Peace Corps sterilize Quechua women forcibly.
The experts in revolution make their peace, relating
at this time to the One-World Crusade.
In Vietnam, in Cambodia, in Beirut,
the revolution goes on.
In Bolivia, the Indians die by 35 in the mines.
Salvador Allende is dead.
Pablo Neruda is dead.
The revolution is over.
Somewhere.
The turn is up.
The clans are coming in: Bear
Bow, Lizard, Parrot, Oak, Flute, Wolf, Fire
Earth Sky:
The buffalo dance
underground.
The blue star dances in the center of the village,
in the center of the heart of the people,
the heart of heaven, underground.
Hurucan,

Gucumatz,
Quetzal,
Ciacahuatl
sing, underground.
The past will speak to the future
underground. Relate to the silence
underground. Relate to the legends,
underground. Telling
the stars of midnight
where to go.
The melted flesh of Indios
sings the death songs in the revolution of eternity.
These are the furrowed ground.
The field of revolution.
The seed of spring.
Wound
of memory.
Wound
of time.
Wound
of conscience.
With knowledge.
With Bolivia,
land of fabled mines.
With Cambodia,
land of fabled mines.
The blood of the people fertilizes the earth.
The revolution goes on. Denied by experts
in a common cause, it still goes on,
the blood still flows

the flesh still melts
the clans still come in
the light still dances in the Center
in the heart of Kawaicomu
in the universe of tomorrow
in the spirit dancing now beneath the Plains.
Locked in loneliness
the new life begins.
And all the experts in the universe
can't stop its round.

Spires

leading into purity
must not be contained—
sort it out:
beans for the pot,
clothes for the load
dimensions for utterance
what ever it is
that must be said
say it
goddammit
straighten the broken roads
mend the sherds with careful glue
obliterate
the opposing hills.

Waiting for a Ride

Evening swiftly descending—
space ship banking to land, save
us on an unfamiliar world. On the asphalt
small cars move over, taking used bodies home.
And evening moves quickly,
(arrow of immensity) no
proportions to mar the flight,
swift
landfall
dark.
I watch each moving thing as though it was the first:
the sight of it could be liberation, love beating me,
if I could see any one thing for what
It will never be.

Shadow Country

I walk in from evening, fresh and cool, happy, loud—
sting of fog on my face, in my eyes. The poet tells of woe,
blood and shattered bones on the pavement of his wishes,
childhood splattered all over the floor in broken memory,
and I sit, cloaked in steep mesas waiting for night, so
far from here, and hold to the feel of your hands on my face
like five o'clock thunderheads and cirrus on my cheeks,
cool 10,000 foot fog across my nose and eyes

this is not death. Maggots in the bowl
do not draw me as they draw the poet crying in the mike, his
intensity. The prancing black stallion of *I*
quiet for now in me, in this
shadow country where corpses shuffle to the bar,
get their meaning dry or sweet,
red or white, dark or light, in the pitcher or the glass
to cool their mouths, to sweeten their breaths, to bring
wholeness to their memory, gone like smoke, like knowing for sure
how it was yesterday.

Behind my eyes,
beneath my hearing,
I know you feeling the wind,
fingering silence and sound as though you could measure

their significance, winnowing like Circe with the breeze
and I stop my ears, my thoughts,
try to discover what it is you do.
I feel the sun putting
its brand on my chest
still scaled and purple-red,
sign of the master,
my heart: the Southwest furthers,
the oracle said
and I taste the cool wet north
where the sky touches the earth
hold myself silent
in the posing late night air—
knowing sun and dark
side by side.

The Return

memory
gold
the sun
is wine, the air
a flowering (deep)
I see a cliff
beside it an arroyo
dry and intangible (waiting)
(the ending's clear)
a deer
tall grass whispering
the sky.
(madonna
your mantle
is gentle is
grace and splendor) I recall
the smooth soft white rock
I used to carve
the long ache of knowing
(how I called you arms open to the sky
your name unknown)
high on the childhood mesas I stood
cicada for conversation
wind for companion

juniper for friend.
I made runes
singing
I remember.
childhood an echo on the hollows
of the hills. Blossoms of yesterday
fall from our eyes.
I remember the eternal drought
(how the trees at dusk wrapped
their branches around the light)
still.

Paternity

When father gets into my dreams
he is always kind. Once
I was dying, floating
above his head over the old
Cubero graveyard and he ran
after me, crying.
The light was soft—
dawn or sunset—
mountains purple and deep
in the cool distance
the huge sandstone mesas gold
as he ran under me, crying.

Once we rode horses
under the blooming apple tree.
He led me carefully
telling me not to be afraid.
We rode through a cool park
formed like a Joshua tree
paths branching asphalt through
the green, green grass.
We were going home . . .
down to the small valley
of the adobe village.

I could see the lake glittering
in the distance
and the grass turned to white
sandstone as I watched.
Although the mesa we were
descending wasn't steep,
I slid too fast
out of control
and couldn't stop.

There are pictures of my great-
grandfather, my father's
Jide, grandfather—a small,
straight man with a mustache.
He liked to hunt snakes for fun
of scaring grandma, *Sitte,* with.
Once he got bit and made my father
cut the wound with a knife he'd heated
himself in the fire. He sucked the
venom and cauterized the gash.
Grandpa used to hide his whiskey
under the stairs so *Sitte*
couldn't find it. He'd have
my father fetch it when he wanted
a drink. He never drank
before five p.m., and then drank
most of the night. He gambled
and kept a woman uptown.
He used to dress like a prophet
and peddle rosaries and holy

pictures in Kansas. They thought
he was insane and spent money
to buy his wares from the Holy Land.
He stayed for free at the best hotels.
He used to shoot at *Sitte*
when she was carrying water from
the well for supper.
There are pictures left behind.

In my dreams
my father is always kind.

Recuerdo

I have climbed into silence trying for clear air
and seen the peaks rising above me like the gods.
That is where they live, the old people say.
I used to hear them speak when I was a child
and we went to the mountain on a picnic
or to get wood. Shivering in the cold air then
I listened and I heard.

Lately I write, trying to combine sound and memory,
searching for that significance once heard and nearly lost.
It was within the tall pines, speaking.
There was one voice under the wind—something in it
that brought me to terror and to tears. I wanted
to cling to my mother so she could comfort me,
explain the sound and my fear, but I simply sat,
frozen, trying to feel as warm as the campfire,
the family voices around me suggested I should.

Now I climb the mesas in my dreams.
The mountain gods are still, and still I seek.
I finger peyote buttons and count the stalks of sweetsage
given me by a friend—obsessed with a memory
that will not die.
I stir wild honey into my carefully prepared cedar tea

and wait for meaning to arise,
to greet and comfort me.
Maybe this time I will not turn away.
Maybe I will ask instead what that sounding means.
Maybe I will find that exact hollow
where terror and comfort meet.
Tomorrow I will go back and climb the endless mesas
of my home. I will seek thistles drying in the wind,
pocket bright bits of obsidian and fragments
old potters left behind.

Poem for Pat

I wanted you to hear that song
she told me
so I listened and listened
trying to understand why
even admitting it was lovely
heart provoking
I still wondered
it took me clean through winter
and past full-bodied trees
into another snow.
Well I'll be damned, here comes your ghost again—

It happened to be on the day
we found each other again she said
and we were shivering at what we contemplated
locked together on the sandstone mesa at star rock
we were looking everywhere, she said
diné country spread at our feet
we could hear the coydogs howling far off
and watch the chindi—dust devils
whirl their plans on the floor below
watch for rain.
Our breath comes out white clouds,
mingles and hangs in the air

there were cedars twisted near where we sat.
It was spring.

Today the sun flows softly through my window
and I'm listening to the song,
thinking of her again on that mesa
wondering what mystery materialized out of that wind
and if it rained.

Laguna Ladies Luncheon

ON MY FORTIETH BIRTHDAY

Grandma says it's so depressing—
all those Indian women,
their children never to be born
and they didn't know
they'd been sterilized.
See, the docs didn't want them
bothered, them being so poor and all,
at least that's what is said.
Sorrow fills the curve of our breasts,
the hollows behind the bone.
Three closet Indians
my mother, my grandmother and I
who nobody sterilized. Our
children are grown.
We do not dare to weep
over coffee in this elegant place,
quiet, we hold their grief unborn.
My mother says it's the same
as Nazi Germany.
A medical holocaust.
Now I'm officially
an old woman, she says,
I can tell them that.

Never Cry Uncle

FOR OOK

he liked the ones who would be friends—
the street kind, the hardtimers, the pals:
they were most often black, because he
was indian and there weren't so many
indian faggots around, and those there were—
well, I don't know, maybe he was over them.
maybe he'd gone through them, or,
most likely, they reminded him of home,
a fearful thought;
of his wife, an indian woman,
of his mother, likewise. but not so wise
was he. he kept getting ripped off and bruised.
he kept drinkin too much. he
took too much valium, too much speed, too
much angel dust. too much acid.
too much mescaline.

he went sometimes to the Indian Center. went
sometimes to the powwows, all dressed up
Pueblo Indian style, bandanna rolledup and tied
around his head, thin pale hair drawn back,
ponytail style. earrings, necklace,
icecream pants, velvet shirt, blanket

over his arm. he looked swell.
but it depressed him to go there, even
the fry bread, even the good sweet corn. his
friends couldn't keep him from getting hurt,
they tried. they spent as much time taking
care of him as they could.
and his family—us, his nieces, also exiled,
too far away from blood and home
to make sense. we kept his money when he asked;
we gave him some of it when he asked. we
got him out of jail when he asked. we took
him home. we all finally got tired of it,
though, locked as we were in our own blood
feuds, locked as we were in our own hardtimes
hustles, and streets, and trips, and friends.
he got beat bad, but he didn't die. he spoke
only Spanish instead. he refused
to remember how it had happened. forgot
it all and remembered only Lucky Strikes
and sometimes friends and beer. he got
locked up that way, and that way he got
loose. beat senseless he was,
and left for dead. but he didn't die.
just got locked up again. now he listens
to the hum forever buzzing in his head.
he only makes dumb indian jokes.
he only remembers his hardtimes friends.

El Cerrito, 1984

Heyoka, Coyote Tale

Alfonso's house is gone. There's
a space where it used to be. The
baile hall is fallen down, tin roof
rusted on the ground. The ghostly cattle
dance there now, from the looks of it.
Remember Alfonso? He was obscene. When I was seven
he asked if I would trade him
a banana for a doughnut. I didn't know
what he meant for some time. But
my girlfriend got mad when he said it,
and he leered, so I knew the drift.
He was obscene. I wonder if he's dead.
Maybe his ghost dances in the ruins
of the baile hall with the cows.
And I remember Pinky who had French
pictures the boys of Cubero sniggered over.
He was also obscene, but a lot younger,
and not to be confused with the Anglo Pinky,
the one who brought my uncle out. Neither
of them ever forgot it, and one day Pinky,
the Anglo one, tried to do a blow-job
with a shotgun. It blew him away instead; left
his brains, pink I suppose and probably red,
splattered all over the walls

of the house his crazy old mother lived in alone
after she cleaned up the mess. Until she tried
her son's trick: it worked for her as well. That
house is still there, not fallen down
in the least, its windows covered
with galvanized tin, its dark green cement walls
fading but strong. It's on the road
out of Cubero, just on the edge
of the Laguna Reservation.
We ride past it on our way out of town.

El Cerrito, 1984

Koshkalaka, Ceremonial Dyke

it is a strange world we walk
                                        like strangers
it is said that some are here who are not here
the leavings of the gods—
forces, spinning whorls, whatever
I cannot name but
that I know
you see them everywhere
around, sometimes in the oddest
shapes and places
like in a brambled yard
                                        a single hollyhock
blooming impossibly
(though if it is, then it's possible)
or a plaster of paris figurine
garishly painted
                                        indian chief
a only hollywood cum edward curtis projection
emitting singular grace
on the other side of the wall it hangs on
a plaster of paris chief, imagine—
or a wild cat in the grass behind the shed
incongruity   perhaps
but that it should be

all of some piece—I wonder whose tapestry
what strands, where does the design
                    become perceptible
and as I said, they say that some
there are who are not
except by means of grace,
beings there are who walk next to this world
this room, this place—

you know.
you see them like that
in an angled glance, a between-blinks sight.
do you see yourself also so?
a banana peel dropped carelessly by some
                    shadowed being
left in all likelihood in some path
for some unwary, seeking
bright bits of cellophane or cloth,
a random bit of thread
fallen from some unseen dress?
do you have any idea
                    what you are?

fragments.
pieces of movement that is neither senseless
nor sensible, except in strange droppings
maybe god-spoor
                    tracking.
wilderness is wild, after all.
what gets netted beside some savage stream?

who hovers in the air murmuring some wild call
just to the side of some primal spring?

I know about them. the shadows that sing.
                                                  the pieces.
you read about them all the time.
in some of the strangest places.
did you ever notice how they
won't be kept out? there they were,
caught in a plaster wall hanging, in
the sunwheel caught somehow behind it—
or before it depending on
your point of view—
almost unseen

heyoka time.
                                                  koshkalaka.
ceremonial dyke. another way of making.
re making. initiated means re made.
are the days of *heyoka* coyote? *koshkalaka*?
                                                  (spider the changer)
                                                  (spider coyote)
when the earth turns to mush,
before it becomes ripe, is it
transformational time?
did you hear a flute
in some other distance?
did you feel the passing
of butterfly wings?

when I saw it I couldn't help but wonder:
the light on the stair
(though to be exact
there are no stairs there that I could see)
the old man who kept changing
from uncle to distance
from distance to saint. do you remember,
he showed me how to know
the time. did I see, was he there?
somehow leftover in plaster
painted with garish brush
a child's garden of indian
a transformational device.
                              a meta/phor?
it was before I saw the plaster
of paris saint, I mean, *ugh,* chief,
that I saw the sunwheel, sunshield,
uncle sunchief, who keeps; I know it
as the one sun woman wears when I see her
which was how I knew what belonged
there. did you think it odd
that the walls looked like woods?
a cabin in the forest.
a lodge on the plain.
it was plain, then. and even
plainer when you found the plaster head
hung carefully on the inward wall
the brave mr. buckingham from
my childhood, one of those strange books

my mother always found for me.
the brave mr. buckingham was a brave
indian who kept having accidents
and each time he did, losing arms,
legs, trunk and all, his niece
would feed him strawberries.
the story would always go at that point
like this:
"and the brave mr. buckingham said
'that didn't hurt!'"

even when all he was
was a head set upon a branch
of a neighborly tree
and his niece fed him strawberries
stuck on the tines of a rake
he said it. did you think
how odd.
to see brave mr. chief head
on the paneled wood wall?
I bet when they hung him he said
"that didn't hurt!"
I wonder if he got to eat strawberries.
I wonder if my mr. buckingham is dead.

niecy, niecy, on the wall
whose the fairest of them all?

as my own uncle used to say.
did I ever make it clear about uncles?

mine, for instance? anyone's who is
a leftover from the old
                    woman days?
where no woman is daughter of a man
                    but niece.
one of my uncles is ook. one is oak. another is
indian scout. the last is unnamed.
they all play guide to my perversity,
trickster to my straight.
believe me, I know coyote
                    when I see one.
even when he's got another name.

in time, in time.
whatever is in place at the time
gets to sit down. to go down.
to run to the beach, the stream.
to hover on the edge of the spring—
the one where the womansprite lives.
you know the place; it's leftover from
                    womantimes.
in other times we sat there, weeping.
in other times we danced around
the clear water eye and sang—
or the fire, it's all the same—
making rope babies spun between us
in the ancient ways of our beginnings
our initiations into these things
                    koshkalaka
daughter/warriors,

sister/lovers—metaphor of grace.
in other times you beat me savagely, left me for dead.

do rope babies from another space
turn up in this as plaster indians
from *koshkalaka* plains?
are strawberries inexorable in the tale?
why strawberries? I know.
they are sacred to one of our kind.
galaxy woman.
spider woman.
rainbow woman.
rope-baby queer woman.
changing mystery woman.
strawberry blood woman.
you remember the night we went to her lodge.
they are all the same
woman.
koshkalaka are her daughters.
warriors. initiates. broken ones.
it is all the same.

you find these fragments
in the strangest places,
like I was saying:
manuals for budding initiates
masked as a simple child's book
a book all about Iroquois initiation
(though how could you tell?)
a book about

the importance of uncles and their faith,
given by, taken by, an uncle's niece.
and what the initiator says
to the initiate, when he is magically hung
on a bough, eating strawberries for the last time.
He must have been an Iroquois because Iroquois
like Lagunas walk the strawberry path when they die.
They walk with the shadows into the stars
to that other place, in that other time.

So it's that time, is it?
you see I knew it was,
and that this was how it would be,
how I would be. and you.

San Pablo. October 1984

That's a Switch or So She Said

Duplicity tricks
are firechanged twins
cornstuffed implicitly
old sorceress Mother Earth
locked in lech
catty bitch draws down four lines
switches her
steel tipped nine tails
seven sisters
stories sliced
in cruel proportion

Meantimes
way down INside
wind and time trade places
take each other for a ride
beam and blow change slots
sluts and saints
all the same
blast and get away
her monstrous Twin
grandson gods
don't keep still for anyone

and what I want—
ye gods! you kids
that's what she said
transform for what? to make
wind?

How she blows
the bottom up
lunacy changed for solarity
sobriety overtakes the switch
in which any slot will do
for him, for her
and who's to know
which is witch
in any time, oh
never mind
four by four and texas two
make switch with switches
as any conjurer unused to salt
should care to know

What she said I can relate
because I heard her mumbling
muttering over blasted matters
twigs and pegs and other mothers
moving kids from jar to jar
dip em first in
radiation slime
called vital algae and other finds

stirring blowing blasted brine
kick shit out of em in two/two time
once and none, nuns and two
under parts turning out
inner sides turning up
not just any penny
for her eyes
lettuce, turnips, yes and peas
the three sisters
sacred in lost memories
which's what we said
3 child girls transformed betimes
at the flick of a switch to
hags, crones, harridans—
what did we do?
spindles twirling
crinolines swirling
dextrous feet stepping, making wine
washing blood from balls of twine

The duplex-city
torn in two
electromagnetic pulse
so to speak
charged it to me
care of BIA
and BofA
lurking beneath
declaimed above

on top of that
split level roof
that leaked
and the trick
I knew that quick
a sooth which whips and bakes
lemony fluffed chiffon sweet cake
sometimes makes dill mayonnaise

Sorcery that grandmas know
ye gods you kids is what she said
yes
terday is what you learn
and no tomorrow
without ex change
rites of days
lost her mind
she used it up
a fire and murmur
all the time
forgot in rhyme
what switch is which
witchery born
conjurer hags had that ache
to go as far as grandma's itch
the one she kept between her legs
a duplicitous ticket
that womansimple trick
it cuts in two

sews up anew
in the same way one and one
made particular two

Changelings
shortchanged
seas and mountains
into brilliantblast are
stars that quick
north to south
east to wet
forget forget
is your memory used up yet?
Ye gods! You kids, that's what she said—

NOW YOU KNOW HOW AND WHAT
HAGS BEGET

San Pablo. May 1987

Malinalli, La Malinche, to Cortés, Conquistador

> And among other gifts of tribute the now-subdued people of the Maya coast gave to Cortés their choicest girls, and among these the slave-girl, Malinal. . . .
>
> It was in March 1519 that the people of Tabasco gave the Lady Marina (as Bernal Díaz always speaks of her) to the strangers, and this was in the shadowland country at the far frontier of the Aztec confederacy. . . .
>
> Throughout the first march on Mexico, after they were joined by Malinal, the Spanish were forced to fight in only one instance. . . . Otherwise the road of their first penetration into the country . . . was paved by a string of diplomatic victories as remarkable as so many straight passes at dice.
>
> —WILLIAM BRANDON

Ever I twisted you to my will,
oh great bringer of the goddess's wrath,
for you did not know that she sang
of your victories before your name was dreamed,
before your flesh was formed.
Ah, you marched, brazen and satisfied,
certain of your cunning and your strength,
and of your place before all of the gods,

straight for the heart of my chief enemy,
he who gave his life and gold in fear,
but in certain knowledge of his part:
only you, unblessed conqueror,
father of my son, remained ignorant,
boastful of a power you would never own.
You stride the continents of your fool's pride
not knowing why it is I, Malinche, whose figure
looms large above the tales of your conquests.

The Spaniard has a disease for which
the only cure is gold, you said; nor
did you know the disease was more of the spirit
than of the flesh: you thought to mock
the piety of him who bowed before you,
of him who was my enemy, my companion,
my beloved Moctezuma. He gave you
all the gold you sought, unprotesting.
Did you ever think to wonder why?
Or how it could be that you,
paltry in your barbaric splendor,
alone could ride
across the jungles and the hills
to the heart of Aztlán?
Did you never wonder who it was
that led you in, let you in?
Did you never wonder why?

And I myself have been maligned: a fitting
irony. Maligned I, La Malinche,

chief of traitors, chief of slaves.
Betrayed I the father gods,
the false serpent who claimed
wings, who flew against
the grandmother sun declaring
prior right; who brought
murder and destruction, gold and jade;
who dreamed of war as tribute
for his blood-drenched kings.
And knowing this, still
I prayed to the mother of us all,
she of sun and star who gives
both life and light,
anguished did I pray to the serpent
woman who lies coiled and still, waiting.

The hour is late, Cortés.
And just as I stood
and watched you strip great
Moctezuma of his gold, just as I stood
guiding your words and your soldiers
with my gaze as I had guided them
with my many-flavored tongue,
I now stand, silent, still,
and watch with great Cihuacoatl
as your time runs out.
Listen: in the barrios even now I hear
her wailing cry as it was heard
in the chambers of the ruler a cycle ago:
oh, my beloved children,

where will I hide you?
Look into the holy mirror that you stole
from him, who you murdered for his will:
see if in its depth you can see my face,
glimpse the falling feathers
of your dying king.

Pocahontas to Her English Husband, John Rolfe

> In a way, then, Pocahontas was a kind of traitor to her people. . . . Perhaps I am being a little too hard on her. The crucial point, it seems to me, is to remember that Pocahontas was a hostage. Would she have converted freely to Christianity if she had not been in captivity? There is no easy answer to this question other than to note that once she was free to do what she wanted, she avoided her own people like the plague. . . .
>
> Pocahontas was a white dream—a dream of cultural superiority.
>
> —CHARLES LARSON, *AMERICAN INDIAN FICTION*

Had I not cradled you in my arms
oh beloved perfidious one,
you would have died.
And how many times did I pluck you
from certain death in the wilderness—
my world through which you stumbled
as though blind?
Had I not set you tasks
your masters far across the sea
would have abandoned you—
did abandon you, as many times

they left you
to reap the harvest of their lies.
Still you survived, oh my fair husband,
and brought them gold
wrung from a harvest I taught you
to plant. Tobacco.
It is not without irony that by this crop
your descendants die, for other
powers than you know
take part in this and all things.
And indeed I did rescue you—
not once but a thousand thousand times
and in my arms you slept, a foolish child,
and under my protecting gaze you played,
chattering nonsense about a God
you had not wit to name. I'm sure
you wondered at my silence, saying I was
a simple wanton, a savage maid,
dusky daughter of heathen sires
who cartwheeled naked through the muddy towns
who would learn the ways of grace only
by your firm guidance, through
your husbandly rule:
no doubt, no doubt.
I spoke little, you said.
And you listened less,
but played with your gaudy dreams
and sent ponderous missives to the throne
striving thereby to curry favor
with your king.

I saw you well. I
understood your ploys and still
protected you, going so far as to die
in your keeping—a wasting,
putrefying Christian death—and you,
deceiver, whiteman, father of my son,
survived, reaping wealth greater
than any you had ever dreamed
from what I taught you and
from the wasting of my bones.

Molly Brant, Iroquois Matron, Speaks

> I was, Sir, born of Indian parents, and lived while a child among those whom you are pleased to call savages; I was afterwards sent to live among the white people, and educated at one of your schools; and after every exertion to divest myself of prejudice, I am obliged to give my opinion in favor of my own people. . . . In the government you call civilized, the happiness of the people is constantly sacrificed to the splendor of empire. . . .
>
> —JOSEPH BRANT

We knew it was the end
long after it had ended,
my brother Joseph and I.
We were so simple then,
taking a holiday to see the war,
the one they would later call
the Revolution.
The shot sent 'round the world
was fired from the Iroquois gun; we
could not foresee its round
would lodge itself
in our breast. The fury we unleashed
in pursuit of the Great Peace

washed the Mothers away,
our Lodges burned,
our fields salted,
our Ancient fires extinguished—
no, not put out, fanned,
the flames spread far
beyond our anticipation
out of control.
We had not counted on their hate;
we had not recognized
the depth of their contempt.
How could we know I would be
no longer honored matron
but heathen squaw—
in their eyes, my beloved daughters
half-breed dirt. Along with our earth
they salted our hearts
so nothing would grow
for too long a time.
We had been arrogant
and unwise: engaged in spreading
the White Roots of Peace, we
all but forgot the little ones
dear to our Mothers
and their ancestry,
the tender fortunes
of squash, corn and beans.

Then, overnight, was I
fleeing for my life

across the new borders, my brother hunted
like a common criminal
to be tried for sedition
for his part
among the British. They
lost out just as we'd planned
a century before. But
we had forgotten the Elder's Plan.
So it was we could not know
a Council Fire would be out,
the League unable to meet
in the bitter winter that fell
upon us like the soldiers
and the missionaries,
the carrion birds that flew
upon the winds of Revolution
to feed upon our scarred and frozen flesh.
We had not counted on fate—
so far from the Roots of our being
had we flown,
carried on the wings of an Algonquin priest
we fell into the eyrie
of a carrion host.
Perhaps it is the Immortals alone who know
what turns the Revolution must entail,
what dreams to send to lead us on,
far beyond the borders of our Dreams.
The turning of centuries goes on,
revolving along some obscure path
no human woman's ever seen.

That's how it is with revolutions.
Wheels turn. So do planets.
Stars turn. So do galaxies.
Mortals see only this lifetime
or that. How could we know,
bound to the borders we called home,
the Revolution we conspired for
would turn us under
like last year's crop?

I speak now because I know
the Revolution has not let up.
Others like my brother and like me
conspire with other dreams,
argue whether or not
to blow earth up, or poison it mortally
or settle for alteration. They
believe, like we, that the sacred fire
is theirs to control, but may be
this Revolution is the plan of gods,
of beings Matrons and priests alike
cannot know.

Still, let them obliterate it, I say.
What do I care? What have I to lose,
having lost all I loved so long ago?
Aliens, aliens everywhere,
and so few of the People
left to dream. All that is left
is not so precious after all—

great cities, piling drifting clouds
of burning death, waters that last drew breath
decades, perhaps centuries ago,
four-leggeds, wingeds, reptiles all
drowned in bloodred rivers of an alien dream
of progress. Progress is what
they call it. I call it cemetery,
charnel house, soul sickness,
artificial mockery
of what we called life.

I, Matron of the Longhouse, say:
If their death is in the fire's wind,
let it wash our Mother clean.
If Revolution is to take another turn,
who's to say
which side will turn up next?
Maybe when the last great blast goes up
you will hear me screaming with glee,
wildly drunk at last on vindication,
trilling ecstatically my longed-for revenge

in the searing unearthly wind.

The One Who Skins Cats

She never liked to stay or live where she could not see the mountains, for home she called them. For the unseen spirit dwelt in the hills, and a swift-running creek could preach a better sermon for her than any mortal could have done. Every morning she thanked the spirits for a new day.

She worshipped the white flowers that grew at the snow-line on the sides of the tall mountains. She sometimes believed, she said, that they were the spirits of little children who had gone away but who returned every spring to gladden the pathway of those now living.

I was only a boy then but those words sank deep down in my soul. I believed them then, and I believe now that if there is a hereafter, the good Indian's name will be on the right side of the ledger. Sacagawea is gone—but she will never be forgotten.

—TOM RIVINGTON

1

SACAGAWEA, BIRD WOMAN

Bird Woman they call me
for I am the wind.
I am legend. I am history.
I come and I go. My tracks

are washed away in certain places.
I am Chief Woman, Porivo. I brought
the Sundance to my Shoshoni people—I am
grandmother of the Sun.
I am the one who wanders, the one
who speaks, the one who watches,
the one who does not wait,
the one who teaches, the one who goes
to see, the one who wears a silver
medallion inscribed with the face
of a President. I am the one who
holds my son close within my arms,
the one who marries, the one
who is enslaved, the one who is beaten,
the one who weeps, the one who knows
the way, who beckons, who knows the wilderness.
I am the woman who knows the pass and where
the wild food waits to be drawn from the mother's breast.
I am the one who meets,
the one who runs away.
I am Slave Woman, Lost Woman, Grass Woman, Bird Woman.
I am Wind Water Woman and White Water Woman, and I come
and go as I please. And the club-footed man
who shelters me is Goat Man, is my son,
is the one who buried me
in the white cemetery so you would not forget me.
He took my worth to his grave
for the spirit people to eat.
I am Many Tongue Woman, Sacred Wind Woman,

Bird Woman. I am Mountain Pass
and River Woman. I am free.
I know many places, many things.
I know enough to hear the voice
in the running water of the creek,
in the wind, in the sweet, tiny flowers.

2

PORIVO, CHIEF WOMAN

Yeah. Sure. Chief Woman, that's
what I was called. Bird Woman. Snake
Woman. Among other things. I've had
a lot of names in my time. None of em
fit me very well, but none of em was
my true name anyway,
so what's the difference?

Those white women who decided I alone
guided the whiteman's expedition across
the world. What did they know?
Indian maid, they said.
Maid. That's me.
But I did pretty good for a maid.
I went wherever I pleased, and
the whiteman paid the way.
I was worth something then. I still am.
But not what they say.

There's more than one way
to skin a cat. That's what they say
and it makes me laugh. Imagine me,
Bird Woman, skinning a cat.
I did a lot of skinning in my day.

I lived a hundred years or more
but not long enough to see the day
when those white women, suffragettes,
made me the most famous squaw in all creation.
Me. Snake Woman. Chief.
You know why they did that?
Because they was tired of being nothing
themselves. They wanted to show how nothing
was really something of worth.
And that was me. Indian squaw,
pointing the way they wanted to go.
Indian maid, showing them how they oughta be.
What Susan B. Anthony had to say
was exactly right: they couldn't have
made it without me.

Even while I was alive, I was worth something.
I carried the proof of it in my wallet
all those years. They saw how I rode the train
all over the West for free. And how I got
food from the white folks along the way.
I had papers that said I was Sacagawea,
and a silver medal the President had made for me.

But that's water under the bridge.
I can't complain,
even now when so many of my own kind
call me names. Say
I betrayed the Indians
into the whiteman's hand.
They have a point,
but only one.
There's more than one way to skin a cat,
is what I always say.

One time I went wandering—
that was years after the first trip west,
long after I'd seen the ocean and the whale.
Do you know my people laughed
when I told em about the whale?
Said I lied a lot.
Said I put on airs.
Well, what else should a Bird Woman wear?

But that time I went wandering out West.
I left St. Louis because my squawman, Charbonneau,
beat me. Whipped me so I couldn't walk.
It wasn't the first time, but that time I left.
Took me two days to get back on my feet
Then I walked all the way to Comanche country
in Oklahoma, Indian Territory it was then.
I married a Comanche man, a real husband,
one I loved. I stayed there nearly 27 years.

I would have stayed there till I died,
but he died first.

After that I went away. Left the kids,
all but one girl I took with me but
she died along the way—not as strong
as she should be, I guess. But
the others, they was Comanche after all,
and I was nothing, nothing at all.
Free as a bird. That's me.
That time I went all the way
to see the Apaches, the Havasupai,
all sorts of Indians. I wanted
to see how they were faring. I like
the Apaches, they were good to me.
But I wouldn't stay long. I had fish to fry.
Big ones. Big as the whales
they said I didn't see.

Oh, I probably betrayed some Indians.
But I took care of my own Shoshonis.
That's what a Chief Woman does, anyway.
And the things my Indian people call me now
they got from the whiteman, or, I should say,
the white women. Because it's them who said
I led the whitemen into the wilderness and back,
and they survived the journey with my care.
It's true they came like barbarian hordes
after that, and that the Indian lost our place.
We was losing it anyway.

I didn't lead the whitemen, you know. I just
went along for the ride. And along the way
I learned what a chief should know,
and because I did, my own Snake people survived.
But that's another story,
one I'll tell some other time.
This one's about my feathered past,
my silver medallion I used to wear to buy my rides
to see where the people lived, waiting for
the end of the world.

And what I learned I used. Every bit
of the whiteman's pride to make sure
my Shoshoni people would survive
in the great survival sweepstakes of the day.
Maybe there was a better way to skin that cat,
but I used the blade that was put in my hand—
or my claw, I should say.

Anyway, what it all comes down to is this:
The story of Sacagawea, Indian maid,
can be told a lot of different ways.
I can be the guide, the chief.
I can be the traitor, the Snake.
I can be the feathers on the wind.
It's not easy skinning cats
when you're a dead woman.
A small brown bird.

Taking a Visitor to See the Ruins

FOR JOE BRUCHAC

He's still telling about the time he came west
and was visiting me. I knew he
wanted to see some of the things

everybody sees when they're in the wilds of New Mexico.
So when we'd had our morning coffee
after he'd arrived, I said,

Would you like to go see some old Indian ruins?
His eyes brightened with excitement,
he was thinking, no doubt,

of places like the ones he'd known where he came from,
sacred caves filled with falseface masks,
ruins long abandoned, built secure

into the sacred lands; or of pueblos
once home to vanished people but peopled still
by their ghosts, connected still with the bone-old land.

Sure, he said. I'd like that a lot.
Come on, I said, and we got in my car,
drove a few blocks east, toward the towering peaks

of the Sandias. We stopped at a tall
high-security apartment building made of stone,
went up a walk past the pond and pressed the buzzer.

They answered and we went in,
past the empty pool room, past the empty party room,
up five flights in the elevator, down the abandoned hall.

Joe, I said when we'd gotten inside the chic apartment,
I'd like you to meet the old Indian ruins
I promised.

My mother, Mrs. Francis, and my grandmother, Mrs. Gottlieb.
His eyes grew large, and then he laughed
looking shocked at the two

women he'd just met. Silent for a second, they laughed too.
And he's still telling the tale of the old
Indian ruins he visited in New Mexico,

the two who still live pueblo style in high-security dwellings
way up there where the enemy can't reach them
just like in the olden times.

Yesterday's Child

as I awake, I find me lying,
arm flung beyond the pine bed's
varnished gloss confine,
tears streaming, mouth open—
for breath? for speaking?
and hear me saying in the tangle of my mind
I want my son. I want Gene.

I had been dreaming about him,
the twenty-three-year-old man who is my son,
not about him, really, but about talking
with some woman about him. she was telling me
that I needed to trust, to know he was safe
doing what men do—going about his business.
she was blond with very short tight-curled hair,
teeth broken or chipped, somewhat older than me.

waking, I don't know who she is
or how in the world I could see Gene
who is so far away from me. it was as though
she had a crystal ball, or a closed-circuit t.v.
but only in the mind—I'm not sure whether it was
hers or mine or one we shared

—but I could see him for myself,
see that what she told me was the truth.

still, waking,
finding old tears wet on me,
arm flung barely beyond the limit of my sleep,
understanding stretched
just armslength into the unknown space
the stranger-woman opened up to me,
I remember I am a mother.
I want to see Gene, to talk to him out loud,
see for myself that he's all right,
know whether he has grown
more hair, a mustache, a beard,
find out what he's been thinking about,
who he lives with now, whether
he's working, eating, staying away
from dope and booze and dirty air

as I get up I find me angry
at the vanished son who does not call.

Coyote Jungle

The man across from me
sits tight, holding
together all the plans
of another time,
pointed toe edging
cautious toward a future
of electronic landscape.
Even the forests
have been wired, plugged in
to terminals far away.
He doesn't understand
that the furrow on his
forehead was transferred
from the furrows he once turned
on the land, embedded there
by lightning flash that stunned
him, knocked him silly
as he sat on the tractor
waiting out Nebraska storm.
On that day,
Earth marked him as her own,
and blinded by that light
to tractor hum and rich,
new-turned clods,

he walked to town
carrying nothing but a small
squat black box for doctoring
and a stranger's way of knowing.
Now he sits near me,
squinting into the velvet dark
of technological truth,
muttering with vanished wizards:

DO WHAT THOU WILT
SHALL BE THE WHOLE OF THE LAW

and there casts the enchantment
that will frame our lives anew.
He does not comprehend
the fire-studded darkness
of the words that fall: *silver,*
camphor, mercury, copper, gold,
iron, brass and *lead,* ancient
ritual revitalized on smog-
heavy mountain air.
Jeremiah in the wild,
Coyote hunched on the north-
east border of urban sprawl
he grows sheep and doctors
broken pets;
he builds strong fences
to cradle baby and wife in,
he speaks words to banish
terror in face of the dark

he knows he is facing:
goddam coyotes,
I'd like to see em raise em
in the cities, like
em to see the gutted bellies
of the lambs those varmints
leave behind.

Teaching Poetry at Votech High, Santa Fe, the Week John Lennon Was Shot

I

Crepe paper Christmas,
green and red, turns
and twists, symmetrical,
around the partitioned
segments of the barnsized room—
voices of brown and white young,
rejects from more hallowed halls
on their way to factories in some
nameless and partitioned open space
in the unbending world
of their faceless fate—blend with
mechanical and electronic chatter.
Noise everywhere, scrambling over
untouched books glossy and slick
with disuse. A groan and clatter
of highmigraine screech pulses
unidentified, predictable,
sets my teeth on edge.
My brainends turn, twist,
try to tune themselves
to unpredictability,

to something textured,
recognizable. Still,
I inhabit this slick universe:
hired to teach glossy poetry.
Through their eyes,
I see myself punitive, demanding, irrelevant.
Though I am not
vocationally authorized,
I hold the chalk.

Electronic mornings creep
over my horizon,
fill my days with danger, hang
ominous over the Rio Grande,
chase the mesas north.
On the highway early
driving north from Albuquerque
I saw sunrise gold and dayglopink billow
on the smoke of the electric plant
outside of Bernalillo.
So much beauty in the certain destruction
it spewed into the December crystal air.
Winter settling on the land, a nestling bird.
Stalks of winter-frosted grass
pointed to me my way, made
my pathway clear.
Last night on the late news
they announced John Lennon's murder,
said he died climbing the stairs.
Remembering when I

was on the other side of the desk,
the twenty years between,
I wept.
How had we come to this?
The shots that took him down
spewed a strawberry trail on the steps,
the blood washed away just after
by the city's rain.

II

The best of the world
slumps before me in the room—
minds that eighteen years ago
first turned earthward blinking:
oh yeah.
Wasted.
Turned off.
Tuned in to video narcosis,
stereophonic shuddering light,
in which, transfixed,
these naked angels burn golden pink,
their hopes and mine on dust and booze.
They smirk about "Ever Clear,"
explain when I ask
that it's 180 proof alcohol
unaware of the implications in the name,
of what
another time

the words might mean—
or perhaps not unaware.
There is a certain glint
on each institution-frosted face.
They have grown,
unawares, into electronic commodities,
haven't the will to fight
the mindless nothing that infuses
inexorable anguish into their lives.
Stoned like martyrs of their ancient faith
they go down their days
not understanding
how they've been crucified,
or by who,
they make do with plastic reveries sunk
in heedless desperation.
Synthetic clatter crusts
their days, makes electro-
chemical tissue of their gaze.

What world is this?
Cut off, torn away, shattered, maybe
they dream of when it will get better,
of when they will be free.

III

180 proof.
Neither womb nor honest texture provides

rough comfort or sure throbbing grasp.
Quivering, these desperados
hide beneath sham and sneer,
behind closed eyes, disheveled hair,
stoned on chemicals and beer.
What do they become, these children,
the same age as my own,
who I watch staggering into life,
despair rising
brown and stinking within their eyes
like poison on the desert air?
It billows gold and pink
around their faces, their helpless heads:
They do not plan, they do not dream.
There is no future they can bear.
I want to cradle them,
murmur to keep them from knowing
what I fear.
I will not let them see me weep.
I will fight with them instead,
sneer and rage.
Tell them to be quiet, to sit down.

IV

No munchkin voices. An English
sharpwood point breaks with a smug tap.
Muffled sounds rise in my ears,
the bite of lemon fills my nostrils.

They pass it around, juice sticking
to their hands. I am surrounded
by eyes that canny and closed
measure me, gaze surreptitiously
from faces no more than
nineteen years old.
Artificiality-induced
boredom barely masks
their scorn of the dusty
plastic tiempo their minds are frozen in;
barely differentiated into carpets,
chalkboards, partitions,
desks, shelves, jackets, slacks,
glossy animal posters on the walls.
They understand
the nature of their punishment.
They do not understand their crimes.
They sit behind plastic faces
barely differentiated into closed
and empty, resentful and dazed. They
are sick with disuse,
plasticized in atrophic rage.

V

Touch skin:
one's own
dewy with petrochemicals
soft for now.

Remember wood
gleaming and warm
accepting you—
smells and oils,
polishing.
Handle plastic
that refuses to recognize
whatever it is you are,
huddled into petrochemical clothing
acrylic
cold
unrewarding
no energy in it.
Know the exact dimension
of a dying soul.

VI

Tired.
Week nearly done.
Mind a tree,
peeling dead bark
littering the ground,
waiting
for the last molecule
to be released.
This rubble of ash
shaped into glazed and battered blocks
forms the walls, grey because they are

held together by despair.
Roughshod voices ride
the lockerlined metalclanging corridor.
Eyes glitter on the brink
of suicide.
The principal stalks the lateday halls
the tiny snackbar beyond the farther door.
He collars those who loiter
in these dispirited halls,
haranguing, ordering. His brown face
looks siempre tired.
His familiar Chicano body sags slightly
into his next word. He knows
what he sees. His limp loose tie
bespeaks discouragement, fatigue.
The students allow his harsh
ministrations, pretend to obey
until he is out of sight down the hall,
then return to loitering,
neck halfheartedly, play pinball
on a slightly sagging machine.
Two o'clock.
Ten more minutes and I'll be free.

I teach the students lost
to plastic rugs and desks,
watch silty minds
grainy to my touch's thought,
ooze helpless to the glazed acrylic floor.
Before me one young face

reflected in hand-held glass
gleams.

VII

Wood steel over emotional motivation sullen firetaste smoke harsh hash herbs gross green bitter lemonpeel coffeegrounds awful seeds like wood burning nutcrust walnutskin goats milk the aftertaste liquidy resin kumquats sour cherries sharp a tar burn tongues fire stream chill flight harpoon spiraling tight grapefruit tangy bite spaced torn from shoots green apricots sour blackberries grogged air kind of asleep stomach hurt chest sorry full tingle muscle pulse pulse pulse speed to flight adrenaline spike taking off meadows rise in pleasuring thick as sour cream rancid cheese fresh milk from fat dusty cows taste of blood coats warm throat what do we do with the hole that's left staggering bleeding on the steps ripe ripped on the powered air stale burning rising incense nicotine sweet fingers nauseous air content powdered sugar hills stiff grass pointing billowing into blood the pain a mom ent only gone fish ride lakes na'more clear defined strawberry place rising a stair plas tic fields silent time grows in cement cracks soft fiber fall a feather of breath lemon air

VIII

Around me
the faces are forests
retreating into snow they
whisper about taking her down
giggle defiance . eyes
prepared for punishment
because they KNOW, in carnality
(¡oigan! ¡carnales!)
My words fall on history-reddened ears
She? / He? Who is it that speaks?
"See, man—I mean ma'am (smirk)
You know HE'S talking to HER
because the Beatles are male, man,
and HE says:
let me take you down"
(leering at the thought).
(Dying at the shot, yeah, man,
he's been taken down, *verdad.*)
They do not mention the tone of grief.

Winter here. We wish for spring.
For ease maybe somewhere
for running across fields
forever alive forever free
in some packaged plastic freeze-
dried recurrent fantasy.
But red with the ridicule of self-abuse

in front of me their postures are
vaguely fused to the carmine blaze of rage
that right to the quick bites deep,
touches me in that secret place
where no one dares to go, not even me,
though I KNOW
that inward lifelong sentence, that
single thought that holds
a life in matter's field,
that now bruised and icy bleeds
sweet juice red as ripe berries
on the forever frozen grass

IX

The noise and clutter
of each separate day
fuses into sound:
learned in grit
in multidecibel shriek, we
learned to say what there is to say
under bricks, under rubble of dead
elephants' dream
transformed into heaps of ivory
hedge against inflation
learned that daddy won't come home

he was never there anyway
to take it step by step

like one child stepped
(how many years ago)
trying to get home
scrambling among words
groping for comprehension
among the sneers alongside the tears,
cut off in the smoke of winter air—
a life and a not necessary death
sufficient for that time—still, quiet, dead.

Later that day it rained.

Something Fragile, Broken

1

i had seen something
i had wanted

and sorrow is not to enter
into it:

a sparrow falling: a tiny
fragile egg, crushed

it was in the grass then
fallen, dead.

reached out, that hand,
palm open, such care

fallen anyway, all the way
to the ground

where it smashed.
the slate stones that ringed

the lily pond of my grandmother
held it, blue and broken.

sorrow was not to enter
into it. but it did.

and i am not stone but shell,
blue and fragile. dropped,

i splatter. spill the light
all over the stone

nothing that can be mended.

2

sorrow was not to enter this

but it did. and i
was not to weep, or

think such things or
let you see that this,

which was not to be entered,
was born and broken before

entering. not in tears
exactly, not fallen in

that way, but still.
and i knew what would not

be spoken. a circle that
would not be broken

shattered anyway, or died.
like ripples on the lake,

when the stone has sunk
deep beneath the surface,

die. sorrow has no part
in it. some things just

don't go on. some circles
come undone. some sparrows

fall. sometimes sorrow,
in spite of resolution,

enters in.

Dear World

Mother has lupus.
She says it's a disease
of self-attack.
It's like a mugger broke into your home
and you called the police
and when they came they beat up on you
instead of on your attackers,
she says.

I say that makes sense.
It's in the blood,
in the dynamic.
A halfbreed woman
can hardly do anything else
but attack herself,
her blood attacks itself.
There are historical reasons
for this.

I know you can't make peace
being Indian and white.
They cancel each other out.
Leaving no one in the place.
And somebody's gotta be there,

to take care of the house,
to provide the food.
And that's gotta be the mother.
But if she's gone to war.
If she's beaten and robbed.
If she's attacked by everyone.
Conquered, occupied, destroyed
by her own blood's diverse strains,
its conflicting stains?

Well, world. What's to be done?
We just wait and see
what will happen next.
The old ways go,
tormented in the fires of disease.
My mother's eyes burn,
they tear themselves apart.
Her skin darkens in her fire's heat,
her joints swell to the point
of explosion, eruption.
And oh, the ache: her lungs
don't want to take in more air,
refuse further oxygenation:
in such circumstances,
when volatile substances are intertwined,
when irreconcilable opposites meet,
the crucible and its contents vaporize.

Medicine Song

THE HEXAGRAM

I add my breath to your breath
That our days may be long on the Earth;
That the days of our people may be long;
That we shall be one person;
That we may finish our roads together.
May Oshrats bless you with life;
May our life roads be completed.

—LAGUNA PUEBLO

In this room where voices spin the light
making webs to catch forbidden visions
(center that cannot be grasped) climb
ladders that do not reach the sky,
hands do not touch,
glances unmet rise, fall
gracelessly against shadows that hold
the song inside, tongueless celebration
of what is absurd. Light follows dark,
(helpless voices climb) as though
precious life could be so stilled,

as though a flicker of mind could turn
hurt or terror into this night's
entertainment. The woman next to me
clutches knees to chest
shrinks into a corner of the room
as though she could disappear,
gracefully evade the web
that grows around us.

The wall becomes a solid past:
no unexpecteds here her shoulders
seems to say, and hurt that is not hers
feels out the room, voices climb,
spiral, spin toward finity,
sing obstinately.

THE JUDGMENT

On the webbed finger of a water dream
swims one who is named Child of the Lake—
foolish emblem on the bare surface of the dream.
(Finger of time pointed at my face
as though some unheard shame had dowsed my mind)
and this is unexpected. I have known my shadow
lurked just out of reach, but that it should
confront my sight in crystal clarity,
turning into a shadowed burial place,
making of dream absurdity—agh, but I
saw the Katsina's duck-billed face turn toward me,
heard his words, misunderstood their sounding

and became,
as swift as waters bearing him from me,
plaything of a mind half gone.

THE IMAGE

Long (as song so stricken goes)
I've worn the crown of penitence
on my tongue, a layering of cloud
familiar to my eyes
(that is the sign of Katsina-kind)
and long have told the songs
and tales of Kawaik
how I might make of wandering a reason
an image of a sacred ladder I might climb
as earth and water climb to help
the wingless fish upstream.
But in a room of solid sound,
where shame is emblem
and fear its hopeless twin,
the voices that climb upsong
can only make blank utterance
that grows to blind dream.

THE LINES

child of water
desert mind
broken strands floating
on the surface of the lake
still body so small
the damage barely shows

small thing
unable to spin
turn in your death
shadow too stricken to flow
dream in your silent shadow
celebrate.

Albuquerque, 1971

On the Street: Monument

On the day Fuad died the heat
glittered and melted the asphalt; someone
in Cambridge thought Marx understood the plight
of streets and watered poor hearts of brown, black and gold
masses: proletariat, confined to non-photographic modes
of thought.

I remember wondering how I could
not break; whether the butterfly in the shade of Fuad's
carefully concealed grave hole was a sign—and if
anything was ever sacralized. No matter what
ideologies occurred before that time, my
son was dead.
The good do not deserve anything more
than their virtue. The evil
inherit the earth, regardless of what Marx
has said.

On the street
the commonplace is ideologue: so little time
spent hanging out, romantic shadows hide ivied eyes from spit
on the sidewalk, ground-in shit, sickening heat:
a street is going
someplace. Camera stays.
Nothing in the frame has any reason to be.

Indian Blood

All I can think about today
is the ways I've been invisiblized,
passed over, turned away, disappeared.
And your eyes, mother, the burning shine
on them, the flame.
Your skin has grown darker
this year of your blood's disease, lupus,
that unacknowledged for so long
in the ignorance of penitence and unspoken
rage, the denial of unshed tears,
dismissal, absence, flight,
turned you away from the roots of your flesh,
the arteries of your life, a disease
that grew within you over the years
untold.
All I can think about is
the resignation of your hands
caught in your lap, words
caught in your throat, vision caught
in your eyes held still, your eyes, your
years, the words now mine
because we share the blood-raged
halfbreed line.
And well I understand the bitter knowledge

of what may not be said, of what
cannot be thought, that grows within our certain
solitude.
I never wanted resignation
for my lot, never would settle
for quiet chores to fulfill my days. I
was too afraid of silence. I was too
weak to imagine a life filled with duty
and unspent memories. I did not have your strength.
Yet tonight I see that you are not
all right, as I have always imagined you to be—
that much is clear in the fevered gaze you fix on me,
fix within yourself, as the old ones have always
done. Your eyes burn dark and bright, your skin
browns, moving to match the earth tones of your
inmost soul, your life and your children
dismissed in autumn's flames.
No one can see what
we cannot say.

You keep the picture of my son on your wall,
taken alongside the highway outside
of Laguna when he was six, titled: "Laguna, four
generations away." His blonding hair and
clear, amber eyes gaze out through the window
of the open car door that reflects behind him
the pueblo silent on its rounded hill
along with the camera held in the stranger's hand.
That picture is a measure of our lives: four
generations away from the root of his breath—

your breath, that leaves you in pain.
I wonder what you think when you look at that picture.
Do you remember yourself at that age,
bangs cut straight across your forehead
like Sully's are, Laguna-child style, walking
along the path by the lake with your grandma
on your way to the dances? You say she'd dress up in her
best shawl, black with purple fringe, and say
"Come on, dearie" and taking you by the hand
would begin the trek from New Laguna to Old Laguna.
"And when I'd get tired," you say, "she'd pick me up
and carry me the rest of the way."
You have not forgotten as you are not forgotten
either there or here where the air sits sullen on the hills
and remembers the longago clear crystal sweetness
of stars and shadows, of night.

The hills around Los Angeles are soft
in the evening light. The stars
come out as we speak.
Behind the murderous fog as
when we talk, the words humming between us
like old loves, your voice rippling
like muscles over the wires, "I'm
just putting grandma to bed," you say.
I say what I find myself
wanting to say,
that we must hold to the words we have to share,
hold to our stories, for they are what we have.
The roads are turned to asphalt and their

course is changed, as we have changed
and transformed in the crucible of our lives—you, your children,
your grandchildren, me.
We must each remember everything
that has been said. We must not forget
no matter who turns our stories into lies,
our lives into rubble, our blood
into an enemy that kills.

Halfbreed woman, mother, daughter, sister, wife,
the measure of your blood is of your sight,
your limbs, your knowing that is the same as mine:
you did not forget the charge your grandma laid
on you in fear and rage: "Don't forget you're Indian,"
she said, such few words to guard a woman's life.
She knew how you would be moved away
from the necessities of blood, knew
how lost you would be. But, mama, though you go back
to Laguna only now and then, they
remember you, they remember your name.

Los Angeles, October 1981

Life Is a Fatal Disease

sulieaman the aliman the rhythm in my head goes sulieman the
allemagne
comen sie heah bitte, that's what they said in Cubero where I was
raised
tante Anna tante Eda and the other sister-in-law whose name
I can't remember tante someone on the German side of the family

aunt Anna raised ducks and geese, not the ones Sulieman Ali my
son
liked to chase when he was small. she had a pond in dry dry
Cubero
in the years of the drought that stretched out a lifetime
and a windmill to finger the wind that Sully never saw

but he saw some of Allemagne, skipping down the Rhine
in his whirly rainbow cap, bitte this, wiedershoen that,
widdershin, veedersayne, auld lang syne how close
the sounds of Gaelic, gallic, Gaul forever undivided are
that no one ever mentioned to my knowledge anywhere

tante Anna's granddaughter Olivia and Teresa my friend and I
would sit in windmill shade and watch the ducks dive in the mud.
at night aunt Anna'd put us to bed in the loft of the madeover barn
become their house when they came to America

if you can call Cubero that, and we slept on featherbeds, under down-filled
comfort and handmade lace-edged sheets just like in Grimm's fairytales
because when they fled they were not allowed to take money, only
what they had converted to goods, but uncle Julius, the fallen away Jew,
died soon after, Anna left with four kids, one of whom is dead this year

the clouds pile over the west mesa, rain puddles on the K-Mart roof. reflecting
on itself, the sky peers down, unmoving, unmoved, all is still except barely
budding boughs of the aging cottonwood tree beyond my sliding glass door,
Star Trek the Next Generation, and the strange sacred heart of Jesus
calendar announcing, "Gurdjieff died for you sins"

reminds me of something I forget—maybe
tante Anna, dead these several years, who doesn't grace our easter table
with her wondrous German cookies anymore. "Du bist Bobby's braut."

her nephew my uncle my mother's last sib or half sib or brother no one
really knows dead last night. he was named Robert Bruce, Robert the Bruce.

oh where and oh where is my highland laddie gone from el rancho
gallito—
se fue. there is less and less there here.

and more and more of there here wherever it is we are.
wherever you go, there you are, the bumper sticker proclaims, verdad,
so it
occurs that the dead must be wherever it is they are (were) (have
been)
(will be) forever and ever amen

when I was small Bobby the Bruce was engaged to my dad's sister
Izzy
from the Lebanese side of the family, and tante Anna used to say
when she
saw Izzy who was the youngest daughter and taught me to walk
or was that aunt Ada another daughter

taught me to recite nursery rhymes, the Gettysburg Address,
back in the wartime when I was barely two? I've been to Gettysburg
where the
murdered horses still scream. Hans, Anna's elder son,
taught me to waltz new year's 1944 when he was home on leave.

who taught Anna to say to Izzy "Du bist Bobby's braut" longlongago
back in the village near Kaiserslautern on the Rhine where I went
years after she died before Bobby, Kurt, Mama, Ookie the Sid did

our Jewish Indian hero and his braut didn't marry after all. cancelled
the

wedding when he returned from occupying Japan after the Bomb
twenty
years old even though he had brought a whole set of china from there,

and I suppose, radioactivity, though no one even mentioned that.
later he
married a local girl, sister-in-law of Jido's best friend Dave Armijo of
the west
mesa land grant where all those Anglos live. Dave died years before
Jido died
soon after he saw Sulieman thought his son's son's son was born,
forgot or
never knew Sully's brother Fuad my heart was dead

Jido got mixed up a lot by then. Bob and his other braut wed in
grandma's
garden on the Laguna/Scottish side, next to the lily pond, on the
green lawn
near the arbor groaning beneath the weight of bridal wreath, beneath
the
weeping willow tree, weep for me, and someone sang love songs the
names I
can't remember

but I remember the songs, the ladies in filmy huge brimmed hats, a
garden
party in Cubero where a Jewish Indian married a lost daughter of the
Armijo
family from the old New Mexican side of the family.

in Cubero outsiders make a strange clan, connected by blood, proximity,
shared events, history, fate. comadre, compadre, primo, amte,
guwatze, how
are you and oiga! que pasa, qu'estas'ciendo, dude! Odd sounds and
tones that

later made me sing to Sully the boy of wilderness, Solomon the wordy
wise
who must have brought me to it though he could not speak
for I've not made funny punny word-song lullabies before or since
except for some strange reason just today.

anyway Bobby had horses, windmills, great earthen dams and steel
tanks
where I learned to swim, and real estate in Cibola County the fabled
land
everyone travelled to find back in the times before history came out
west to
find goldless people already here

Izzy had kids, jazz, and a steakhouse in the Big Q
and golf widowhood which was practice for the real thing,
and keeping books like she learned in Cubero when I was two and
three

and everyone would never die, and keeping up with the family—
the one on the Lebanese side, the one on the Italian side,
fixing homemade pizza and kibbe, buchilato, biscochitos, marmoul,
apple pie, corresponding with her once upon a time these years.

last time I saw Isabel was the day Wendy on the Lebanese side though his
father was German American from somewhere in the east died too young
no, at her birthday when pop picked a fight with the dude serving us. today
uncle's gone, aunt's widowed for I can't remember how many years.

tante Anna's son Kurt died a year or so ago, my mom the year before,
granddaddy her immigrant German stepfather years ago about the time
my daughter was born from the Lebanese side of the family until I was forced
to flee to the Big Q for her life and mine from Grants, Cibola County
where all the gold was yellowcake, glowed in the dark

and on our skin like pollen upon butterfly wings, from whence I fled
and now most of that part of the family is dead and I'm a widow, a gay divorcee
getting older, glowing more and more like plastic Mary I had in the fifties
when I was young and only one or two had died and I'd never been to a
funeral and the apple tree was still alive.

ash wednesday's coming on ashes to ashes, dust to dust
not in tante Anna's peaked roof barn of a house she kept
over all the years, tending its vegetable garden just out the back door
an outhouse for a toilet because she thought it belonged outside
with the windmill, the ducks & geese, the pond.

at her funeral in the Big Q the strange minister praying over her
Lutheran
remains told god about Anna the sinful so he would forgive. I
grinned—I
couldn't help it and no one could see—a woman lost thousands of
miles from
her Rhineland village, Christian braut of a Jew who fled into the desert
of mesas, hovering peaks, eternal sky

in all those years in the Cubero of her life never learned English or
Spanish
so couldn't speak except to her kids. imagine tante Anna sinning
speechless, standing at the stove while pleasing Satan with beating
sugared butter into fine flour to feed the family the world on Easter
day

sulieman the allemand, sulieman ali the man who writes buttery
tales of sinless grins, greets people "Grossgott!" with satirical salute
fist pounded against brow left foot stamping loud the floor the
ground
and never sins and isn't dead like the spring,

like his tiny brother all these years is dead
one of my earliest loves to go and leave me here
or Bobby Shaftoe who went to see, to sea, after an attack, last night

no association is ever free

lucky lucky Bobby. lucky lucky Anna. lucky lucky ma. Lurt, Gene
Lebanese

the conquistador from Mora whose last name in English means black snake.
grandma. Ookie the Sid. Johnny Canzoneri of steaks and jazz.

Fuad whose name means my heart. granddaddy, German immigrant who
fought the Kaiser and his own brother in the first world war. uncle Lee
Hanosh sang Lebanese high-songs in Arabic the wondrous at christenings and
weddings and his brother Joe played the derbukke
I haven't heard since Amo died

and primo Wendy dead with Jido, Sitte, Haula, Zahia, Josephine, Pauline,
everyone except Naphie the oldest daughter on the Lebanese side,
Izzy, Ada, Liás—spelled elias but everyone here says it wrong, my dad
on the living side, Cecil

Rose Fidel who was hardly that, Hanna, her husband big black snake. say no
ill of the dead which is almost everyone I used to know when I was young,
and dead was something only grandmas did, Mina my dad's mom, Sitte,
grandma Gunn on the Laguna side. now everyone goes into the arroyo, onto
the faraway sea including Cubero, the sweet water spring, the apple tree

kifik. grossgott. everyone. and synce ye're gaun, vaya con dios.
tante Anna and Bob the Bruce's family's name was Gottlieb
god dear or maybe dear god.
saalem u khalem, du-wih shatz, mine schatz

Albuquerque, 1994

Apache Warrior—Apache Troop

. . . zone reconnaissance
state of the art—tank—
stabilized sight, stabilized gun
15 to whatever miles an hour
bouncing along like this
23 tons of steel wrapped around
a marvel of new engineering
blows you away

Kiowa helicopters
low flying skimming not far in the dust above maybe 50 feet
survey in front of the tanks maybe six miles out
but usually closer
first taste of battle, first blood
the reporter says
the camera sweeps over
lines of armored pumped young men
making their way across the Iraqi desert
Third Infantry, Seventh Cavalry

at higher speeds they fire more accurately
they carry classified numbers of shells
armor piercing some of them
high explosive some of them

are you scared yet?

Crazy Horse Troop
just ahead, Bone Crusher just behind,
flying reconnaissance for oncoming tanks
the Warriors in the Seventh Helicopters
two women fly
one a West Point graduate who survived 20 rapes
thinks it's a real hoot to be the first to see
the enemy,

I can just imagine
Rommel in the desert but you couldn't do it then
there were no WARRIORS in WWII
they couldn't talk to each other real time,
no night sights, no moving shots,
couldn't flee and fight at the same time

things are so different now
you wonder how they got through
but they did,
they were
through, that is
maybe because they couldn't see

none of us really knew the plan
if any of us really knew the plan
if we could just get there quickly
establish a beachhead there

in the oldest desert of western man
the movement across the desert
the oasis of war
as old as the sands
we thought we knew the plan
but they didn't do what we said they'd do

what they said they'd do
Washington said
you aren't following the plan

you don't have a plan,
the commander snapped
and that was true

Tomahawk missile up, up and away, shot
by the photographer bouncing on the hood
of the Warrior as he takes these historic pictures
for the historic Seventh Cavalry
Captain somebody from somewhere Texas
you all come out of there with your hands up like Sheridan said

this commander's precursive self said chasing
other heathens in fields of blood and buffalo grass;
this one 26, 27 maybe, never in battle before—
and those 18, 19 year olds he leads
all wound up, adrenaline high, MRE,
no sleep, only the desert and the threat of gas,
nightmares of World War I, the corpse and rat filled trenches,
although postmodern warriors lie in single holes all suited up.

It's crowded and close in there and who knows how many
more days to go
we're just doing what's right the baby faced warrior claims,
like we've always done since so long ago.

"Garryowen" was Custer's marching song
has always been the Seventh Cavalry's

them who were wiped out by the Sioux
in different times of course, defeated then
like to be defeated now, say "Garryowen,"
the Seventh will respond,
HOO HAA

is that from Texas, or Gary, Indiana,
or maybe all the way from Geronimo's grave?

The most important thing when the shit goes down
it's good to have something good to hold on to
a unit with a proud history you can write home about
a motto, a battle cry of your own

I bet when they began to move troops into Iraq
at the cessation of their apocryphal "Shock and Awe,"
some Commander said into his microphone
Heads up, people. We're going into Indian Country.
That was how they began the invasion of Kuwait a decade before.
And in battle after battle preceding through two centuries.
Why not this decade, this century too.

March 2003

America the Beautiful I

compose
discompose
decompose
recompose
expos
expose
indispose
overexpose
predispose
preexpose
propose
reimpose
suppose
superimpose
superpose
transpose
underexpose

when you take a position, even assumptively
you might find your disposition presumptively
supposition suppository; suppose
that's because what you have on deposit
has probably been deposed
say, hey! reposition the composition

hid it in the repository
that's stashed in the depository
so when they posit this new approach,
make propositions and find new topics to broach,
you can bet they have a preposition
way beyond your wildest suppositions
which of course shows them preposterous
which is what they leave to posterity
beyond the reach of obfuscation, iteration,
bodacious boisterous imposture's repository

L: *pausa*: to stop; to rest;
in some of them, from *ponere*, to put: e.g., depose, to put down.
    (pony up, dude)
depose, dispose: L. *prae positer*; before-put and/or down-put,
out-put the dog
place, placement, order, organization + prepositional sites of these;

rhymes with pose
arapahos; navajos; anglos; buffalos; jingoes; manifestoes;
pueblos; shalakos; ufos; chicas y chicos; todos los pendejos

Fort Bragg, 2004

America the Beautiful VII

it's the petunia of the spirit that remains,
along with noble phlox, tenacious lobelia,
stubborn dandelion, small cedar, scrub oak.
the streets today are hot in this little town
going big time. new crosswalks,
high rents in this worker's paradise
where labor's cheap and gas costs high.
we live on the rocky shores of earth's greatest sea.
where the earth's greatest pines used to grow,
where rhododendrons bloom like giant trees of light
providing opportunity for one and all to take
the easy way out—one bright petal salad
and you're gone. well-bred roses here are grown
in pens to keep out deer (although wild ones bloom free).
here as elsewhere I've learned that when white-out fluid
thickens it mucks up the line, blurs the print:
I know that rivers can get that way too.
surely you remember the nations' vow:
as long as the rivers flow?
(surely you don't)
and more, they vowed: as long as the
grass grows. sometimes I long for
begonias, daffodils, honeysuckle, lilacs
out of time I like the way they

set off neon and honky-tonk
highlight scat and rap. make a statement
with bluegrass and blues.

in the center of our town there's a trophy:
I saw it only by accident though it had been
there for more than a hundred years
maybe less. A huge chunk of redwood trunk,
huge saws mounted against its vastness,
as though to say: look what hungry
family men armed with steel can do.
the dead-tree bisected by the steel that downed it
guards the mansion that's now historical site
where photos of leading townsmen
longago hang . . . not one hungry family man,
all well-fed, stern, sleek . . .

beneath the new surface of trendy shops
and friendly folks invisible war is waged:
war on red woods, war on red
people, war on poverty
and impoverished, war on drugs,
war on war. there must be a place
for free range deer
for grass growing wild and free
for lobelia and fuchsias, for deathly
rhododendrons, for longing and rage
in this place of seven thousand
mad whited-out souls and three
hundred mad indians nobody recognizes.

just look around and see what is now, what
should be, could have been, what's the use.
there is reason enough for indians to go mad
whited out over centuries, for water
to get sullen and refuse to flow. for
grass to sulk. even the sky is crazy with rage.
even the earth's gone mad.

Spring 2005

America the Beautiful XV

here it is—our last chance:
saloon hotel gas pump
                                                  before the grueling
                                                            mohave
desert dwellers including
Saddam are not
                              disarming
any oasis can be
          startled
                                  a
                              wake
                                                  ning dream

game OVEROVEROVER
(tomorrow
(another week or two
(a month   max

          remind
          s me of the fifties
          family and drive west every year
          (or as many as daddy could
                                                  take

[FLAGSTAFF ARIZONA]

three a.m. Headed down to the desert
to arrive before dawn. it wasn't the end of
anything then, Y'all come out of there
with yer hands up
'cause nits breed lice notwithstanding

—we pretend never happened—

(no cold war along that lonesome hiway
(no atomic bombs no
        air-conditioned cats
        no four-lane freeway
        mother make her stop
        move over you fat pig
                california here I come sewanee
                blackbird bye bye

our squabbles fill the empty miles
driven through the killing heat
hollering *if you ever plan to motor west*

        DON'T

SQUEALING WITH HILARITY AT OUR WIT
faces crazy red and swollen

YOU KIDS! QUIET DOWN BACK THERE!

Heading into the blazing
high noon sun
do not forsake me oh my darling
(mohave. joshua trees. lizard in the grass.
there's no grass dummy
Inyo, Twenty-Nine Palms, Salome-Where-She-Danced
(nobody mentioned her taunting the saint
"the Dance of the Seven Veils" (parents grin in
the front seat

I can almost hear Uncle Joe playing the derbukke
Uncle Lias chanting high Arabic
in the crowded car the rising heat
all day I face the barren waste
the bloody head of the saint—
I found out later high school now

I wonder:
maybe
the fanatic saint looked like Saddam or
like my dad who if he had a thick mustache

would

(look

like Saddam

who might

(look like Mar Hanna come again

if Saddam or my dad never shaved——who knows?

I'm the Sheik of Araby

played at the Casa Marina every time biye, daddy, entered

(talk about the last chance hotel—

bartender, desk clerk, whore and all

closed down tight for day

opened only nights

nobody mentions the ladies of the night

[BARSTOW]

climbing climbing

out of the dry dry sea

engine heating almost over

heating

swoop down Sierra rising from sea beds on each side

towering high as waves at the beach tower

[SAN BERNARDINO]

glide

glazed

into smog rich air

i still believe is the happy-ever-after-smell of

[CALIFORNIA]

all asleep on the broad back seat
tired of going
tired of singing
tired of squabbling
tired of laughing

how deep is the ocean
we're on our way to somewhere
I'd like to leave it all behind   and go find

BURMA SHAVE

i can't give you anything   but love   ba-by

past anticipating
ready to wait
ready to get out and play

cool, clear water

let us pray

BOP BOP

America the Beautiful XVI

Rendering to Caesar what is Caesar's and to god what is god's
I watch cnn moneyline and listen to some opera on cd player via my pc.
Rendering to Caesar even the language I choose, the part of god
is the moment I am struck and pause. Silence. Chest fills
Eyes grow tears. Still.

I found the cd in a pile of stuff. Its title, *The Greatest Show on Earth.*
For months it sat on my desk waiting for the time I would check
it out.
Today I was needing desk space. It's Christmas, nearly so. The news is
obnoxious. And the sounds of Caesar everywhere
bring me neither peace nor cheer. Even the deer don't know what
time it is
it seems; not one wears antlers. Not one has a glowing red nose.

I don't know who is singing. There is a line in a song the title of
which I do
not know, although I recognize the melody, the soprano rendering
her aria.
Tosca? Carmen? The last word, co-*si,*
Sticks in my brain and in my sinews, old and drooping as they may be,
growing tangles as my hair grows thin. There are moments
driving near the ocean watching the surf pound its way inland

or listing in on the soft gossip of the great trees that I will
remember,
The pause, then,
Co-*si*.

Fort Bragg, December 2006

America the Beautiful XXX

FOR GENE AND LAURALEE

Long sun shining on the west fork of the Dolores,
which means sorrow although it was a beautiful place.
Do you remember? Midsummer evening
where your dad hooked his fill, casting a line
out on the wide, swift rush, light slanting long across the flow,
approaching darkness leaning from the high peaks on either side,
deepening to dark the rushing cold where vibrant trout
jumped joyful for the last glittering bits
of light? He grilled his catch
dipped in cornmeal and oil
as around us grew silent the soft whispering chill of night.
Happy next to the kerosene stove
in the pool of hissing kerosene lamplight,
we warmed ourselves and ate the succulent dead.
Beyond the peaks, so far, the stars burned flat and helpless,
temporarily strung out on nothing,
so very bright.

Fort Bragg, Winter 2004

America the Beautiful XXXIV

macular degeneration
pissing on the NDN nation
whatever happened to live
and take whatever comes
and give back all of it
whatever became of mesas
soldiering on into the blue beyond

whatever happened to make
hurt, death, pain, fear
all we care about when surrounded
is beauty peace and harmony
flower sea coast village picturesque
little traffic quiet birds sly and whole
fish going about millennia
along with their sister rocks sand
salty surf, heavy seas,
keep your eyes covered
when you go out

keep your heart covered
when you walkabout
keep your tongue and your hands
to yourself

keep your head
hold your water
when does it end
where will it begin
I could do without my sight
as long as there was nothing to see
I could do without my life
as long as there was nothing to be
I could do without my heart
as long as I live or die as me
I want the NDN nation
to have another revelation
dance the old dances
sing the elder sings

Fort Bragg, 2004–2007

values

(WITH THANKS TO HENRY REED)

right now we have the value thing. in the past
we had vision. later maybe
we will have shame, guilt, rage, grief. but right now,
right now we have the values thing. hummingbirds
dart about like jewels on invisible wings
and right now we have the value thing.

this is the word of Jesus. and this
is the law of Jehovah, whose work you will know
in his wrathful fires and this is the resolve
of the C.E.O. in D.C. which in our case we didn't choose.
the deer wander quiet over the rise, grazing on whatever's there,

this is the situation: grave in the extreme.
redemption can only be gained by pulverizing waves
of stealthy bombing. please do not try to find haven
in laughing, dancing, waving angry signs. you must
realize that selective massacre is our god-fearing choice. the
daffodils that cluster in the tiny sanctuary just beyond the fence
give no thought to their salvation.

and this you can see is the reason: god is good
and evil is what we despise. the value

of a just war is manifest: to free the enslaved, to heal
their pain and to load them on the value train of salvation.
a huge, fat bee probes a shadowed cluster of purple blooms
repeatedly piercing tender light spilling centers with surgical strikes.
this is called liberating pollen for the hive

we call it liberating pollen for our lives; it's hard
to think about, harder for us to do, but god has commanded:
there but for me goes the least of you. the path has been made clear
by Jehovah, Jesus, Paul, born again President who thinks he's a king,
hierophants who lead us in righteousness, which in our case
we didn't choose. at dusk the birds make their steady way home
to nestle and mumble into sleep as the silenced world flows into dark,
and today we have the value thing.

Still Crazy

It was then as it is now
just as the holy men say
although they took that page
from the Book of Old Wives Tales.

Whatever. I say it works
the same now as it did then
even with all the proud
information that dangles—free radical
deconstructing our realities
that made the world seem solid
since before our time.

Then, was I in that thirty-second year
when one knows little enough . . .
except I wanted the ugly, the unpleasant,
the vicious to just go away. I thought
wishing and willing would make it so.

I got pregnant that summer, nineteen seventy-one

Ecstatic in the full-bodied sight and sound
of the great thunder kachina
like gods they were

towering golden in the sky
high above Gallup
New Mexico.

But the winter I was thirty two
I was smack up against truth:
crippling effects of pregnancy,
six weeks in bed, birth
of blessed twins full of light
one dead two exact months after his birth.

There I was, feeling secure,
believing that one god, one man, one world
would make of everything good enough for me—
even the pain

I had no idea what pain could be.

Fort Bragg, 2002

Self Portrait and a Wish

I don't much go for action,
the speedy joke, quick, sharp wit—
don't go straight toward the goal.
I am an old Laguna Pueblo Indian—poet
ADDle-brain, raised good Catholic girl. I
hover around the edges, discern
shadowed shapes in between. I
like my lighting indirect—
think sun is brutal, seek
the blessed shade. Being so,
I lie in wait, a sedentary bitch.
I have ditch water in my veins just
like the US Senator over a hundred years ago
accused Pueblos and the Spaniards who had lived
among them four hundred years—but how
I wish I was action-packed, loaded for bear,
right on kind of girl.

March 2004

SE FUE [He Left (Himself)]

FOR GENE

A month. And some days.
Losses mount in my drying yard.
Along with the grass, mare's tails,
coastal plants whose names I don't know,
there are the birds.
If I keep feeding them they come.

Somewhere others will be laughing—
dancing, getting drunk, *musicos* serenading them
among the graves. Somewhere
la gente will mount marigolds, before the photos of their dead,
light candles, set out photographs of *los muertos,*
strategically place bottles of booze,
plates of *pan dulce,* other blooms on the *ofrenda.*
The marigolds will fall in a tumble all the way
to the open door. *Bienvenidos.* Welcome.

You used to tell outlandish tales
or play your songs murmuring
over the strings until you had me
in tears. I don't know how
to dance with the dead, or offer

tequila, marigolds, *dulces,* sweets.
But I can say, *mijito,* my son.
Come home.

Fort Bragg, 2003

Minding the Gap

over Noyo Harbor they're building something
maybe it's an extension of the bridge.
I heard a rumor to that effect before
I moved up here. bridge is good;
it's harder to get from here to there
without one.
the bridge they're working on
spans the gulf
between there an here;
seagulls and seals like being there,
turkey vultures hang close by.
lovers and other seekers
stop on the cliffs it spans
just around the cliffs' curve along the waterside
I used to be a bridge from here to elsewhere—
had no idea that bridge-being entailed
lifting here, reaching there,
prop it on your hip up and over you go,
hang over thin air and never tire;
the ones who crossed me were mostly
oblivious. I didn't mind
I minded a lot
few notice a bridge, where it begins,
where it ends, how much faith it implies.

intent on destinations,
what stretches between is a means whereby.
seabirds circle, land, sit on the rails
meditate on fish
humans pass them by.
weighing tons, we swish our way over thin air
a hundred feet above water,
hunched over steering, radios on blare.
just now changes coerce attention; we decry
inconvenience, delay, unsightly cranes.
sometimes amazed and always a bit scared
I drive nearly a half ton of me across the gap,
sometimes quick, sometimes slow it's a matter
of faith I say—in engineering, in construction,
in at least one dead man's body
entombed in the piling—
that they work together to hold up the sky.

March 2, 2004

How Near, How Far

A fine spring day in the East Bay.
The first this year. I am preoccupied
realizing exactly that what slouched
toward the White Sands
to be born is grown, already
getting old. I'm driven to get out
while the sun shines
in a calmer city a life away from Trinity,
a place smugly self-satisfied place
from whence it came, a place
where the perfect sun gets tangled
in the branches of predictably ho-hum trees,
where whatever it is that I've
been dreaming lies asleep,
making everything
I recognize a bit too late—
that that's okay. I did find out
what's in a name, by god,
and I gotta say it isn't much.
Still, a good ol' rummage of 50's junk
piled high in a second-hand store's
a trip, listening to adolescent songs, Gogi Grant,
Chubby Checker, Little Richard, Les Paul
and Mary Ford. Look, some Navajo rugs,

prices pretty good; look formica and chrome tables,
monstrosities of my ill-spent youth
as young married in Grants, New Mexico
a generation and a half ago; look,
aluminum glasses that made your teeth ache
when you used them to drink ice tea. It's
a rush, this spring walk through self-recovery land,
though I discover few if any
homey bargains in the heaps.
I'm reminded that whatever glitters
isn't gold, and nothing ever smells as sweet,
however faint the music,
however high the moon.

Berkeley, CA, 1999

ABOUT PAULA GUNN ALLEN

The daughter of a Lebanese-American father and a Laguna-Sioux-Scottish mother, Paula Gunn Allen (1939–2008) was raised in New Mexico on the Laguna Pueblo. She wrote several volumes of poetry, including *America the Beautiful: Last Poems*; *Life Is a Fatal Disease: Collected Poems 1962–1995*; *Skins and Bones*; *Wyrds*; *Shadow Country*; *A Cannon Between My Knees*; and *Blind Lion*. She taught at the University of California, Los Angeles, where she was a professor of English, Creative Writing, and American Indian Studies. The groundbreaking collection of essays *The Sacred Hoop: Recovering the Feminine in American Indian Traditions* is a touchstone of her work as a scholar, and she edited numerous anthologies of Native and women writers. Allen's honors included the Hubbell Medal for Lifetime Achievement in American Literary Studies from the Modern Language Association and a Lannan Foundation Fellowship. In 2023, UCLA's Gender Studies Department dedicated a professorial chair in her memory.

PUBLISHER'S NOTE

When I founded Levine Querido in 2019 it was with a mission to seek out and publish the brilliant work of authors and artists from communities that had been historically overlooked or underappreciated by the mainstream publishing community. I hope that the new work that LQ has helped bring out has brought great pleasure and satisfaction to readers. With ReLIT, we hope to address the further reality that even when creators from marginalized communities did break through into publishing (as Nancy Larrick wrote in an article published on September 11, 1965, the "All-White World of Children's Books") they often faced problematic assumptions about how big a readership their work would attract, and how its value would be counted. Some of those books never reached the full audience they deserved. Many went out of print too quickly. We will search for these buried treasures and do our very best to cast a new light that will allow them to sparkle once more.

ARTHUR A. LEVINE
President and Editor-in-Chief
Levine Querido

RE
LIT